BETTER THINKING

THINK BETTER. **BE BETTER.**

BY RONDA CONGER

Copyright © 2015 by Better Human, LLC

Cover and Interior Design: Arielle Heinonen

All rights reserved. No portion of this book may be reproduced, stored in a retrieval system, or transmitted in any form or by any means © electronic, mechanical, photocopy, recording, scanning, or other © except for brief quotations in critical reviews or articles, without the prior written permission of the publisher.

This book may be purchased in bulk for educational, business, organizational, or promotional use.

For information, please email info@elevatepub.com

ISBN-13: 978-1937498818

Printed in China
First Printing, 2015

Published in Boise, Idaho by Elevate, a division of Elevate Publishin
www.elevatepub.com

To all those who pushed me to think better...
I am forever grateful.

Think better. **Be Better.**

Its simple math.

When you think better, you become better.

Let's elevate our thinking.

Let's challenge our current mindsets.

Let's think better.

Here's to wanting more. Here's to being better.

Love you madly,

Ronda Conger

A man who does not leave his hut will bring nothing in.

– West African Proverb

I am not a product of my circumstances.

I am a product of my decisions.

– Stephen Covey

ELEVATE

is a transitive verb with means to lift up and improve morally, intellectually, physically, relationally, financially, culturally. Elevate your quality of life by improving the quality of your thoughts. Just as an elevator to transport you vertically to a higher floor, your thoughts, words and actions exist to **ELEVATE** you to higher levels.

Use them wisely, and always remember that the only direction worth moving is north.

— Gary Ryan Blair

— SENECA, ROMAN PHILOSOPHER

WELCOME IT.
EXPECT IT.
ANTICIPATE IT.

— DENIS WAITLEY

VIEW CHANGE AS THE ONE CONSTANT IN YOUR LIFE.

WITH-
OUT
HARD
WORK

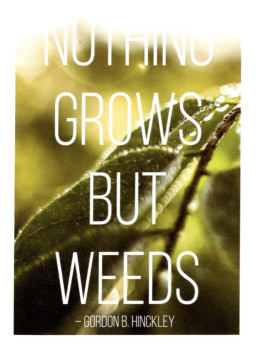

HUMILITY

Humility is one of the most misunderstood
and misapplied words in all of language.
It is about being teachable and
coachable. It implies a continual
commitment to learning
and growing and expanding.

It is living life in crescendo with shoulders back and heads up as we reach and stretch to become our very best, then extend ourselves to help others do the same.

– Excerpt from the book *Aspire* by Kevin Hall

TIME AND HEALTH
ARE TWO PRECIOUS ASSETS THAT WE DON'T RECOGNIZE AND APPRECIATE UNTIL THEY HAVE BEEN DEPLETED.

– DENIS WAITLEY

A man is but the product of his thoughts.

What he thinks, he becomes.

– Mahatma Gandhi

I AM IN *love*

WITH *hope*

– MITCH ALBOM

**Beware of what
you want -**

for you
will get it.

– Ralph Waldo Emerson

DON'T LET ANYTHING STOP YOU.

There will be times when you'll be disappointed, but you can't stop.
Make yourself the very best that you can make of what you are.
The very best.

– Sadie T. Alexander

YOU
THINK
BIG.

YOU GET BIG.

– THE NOTORIOUS B.I.G.

If you rarely give a little more
should you really expect to get a little more?

– Sam Parker

WHICH ONE ARE YOU?
SOME PEOPLE
BRIGHTEN
A ROOM WHEN THEY
WALK IN.
OTHERS, WHEN THEY
WALK OUT.
WHICH ONE ARE YOU?

– COURTESY OF CHRIS WIDENER

The quality of readiness to for and to

If you have good thoughts they will shine out of your face like SUNBEAMS and you will look lovely.

— Roald Dahl

THE MOST IMPORTANT THING IN THIS WORLD IS TO LEARN TO GIVE OUT *love* AND LET IT COME IN.

– MORRIE SCHWARTZ

The foolish man seeks happiness in the distance; the wise grows it under his feet.

– James Oppenheim

Author Sam Lefkowitz remarked, "When asked if my cup is half full or half empty, my only response is that I am thankful I have a cup."

Your life may not be exactly what you want it to be, but you have life. That's something to always keep in mind and be grateful for.

– Excerpt from *SUCCESS* Magazine

**The real rule of
"give and take" is:
before you take,**

you gotta give.

– Jeffrey Gitomer

For all that has been,

thank you.

For all that is to come,

Yes!

– Dag Hammarskjold, Second UN Secretary-General

WHY BE GRATEFUL?

Grateful people are **happy people.**

When you find yourself complaining about something, force yourself to think about the things for which you are grateful.

I write one thing for which I am grateful each morning as soon as I'm awake. I add something to the list many times throughout the day.

If you practice this in your life, you will be amazed by the change in your perspective.

— Andy Andrews

EARNING SUCCESS
IS HARD.

The process is laborious, tedious, sometimes even boring. Becoming wealthy, influential and world-class in your field is slow and arduous. But if you have an aversion to work, discipline, and commitment, you're welcome to turn the TV back on and put your hope in the next infomercial – the one touting promises of overnight success.

– Darren Hardy

OBSTACLES *CAN'T* STOP YOU.
PROBLEMS *CAN'T* STOP YOU.
MOST OF ALL,
OTHER PEOPLE *CAN'T* STOP YOU.

ONLY YOU CAN STOP YOU.

– JEFFREY GITOMER

Accept responsibility for your life. **Know that it is you who will get you where you want to go — no one else.**

– Les Brown

I love trophies, but screw them.
They're for old men, for guys living in memory.

I'm talking about:
Are we competing today,
every minute,
in everything we do in practice.
Are we letting loose
and daring to be great
here and now?
And can we sustain that?
And repeat it.

Trophies are great,
but we're trying to win forever.

— Pete Carroll, Seattle Seahawks Head Coach

NO MATTER HOW MUCH FALLS ON US

WE KEEP PLOWING AHEAD. THAT'S THE ONLY WAY TO KEEP THE ROADS CLEAR.

— GREG KINCAID

EVERYTHING IS POSSIBLE

FOR ONE WHO **BELIEVES.**

– Mark 9:23

My message is simple:

Take control of your life.
— Charles Barkley

I WILL GO ANYWHERE,

PROVIDED IT BE FORWARD.

– DAVID LIVINGSTONE

THE BAD NEWS IS
TIME FLIES.

THE GOOD NEWS IS
YOU'RE THE
PILOT.

– MICHAEL ALTSHULER

A leader's attitude is caught by his or her followers more quickly than his or her actions.

– John Maxwell

Dream big, **WORK HARD, STAY FOCUSED** and surround yourself with good people.

— Author Unknown

THE LAW OF
EXPECTATIONS

I've found that whatever you expect, with confidence, becomes your own self-fulfilling prophecy.

When you confidently expect good things to happen, good things usually happen to you.

If you expect something negative to happen, you are usually not disappointed.

Your expectations have an inordinate effect on the people around you as well.

What you expect from people and situations determines your attitude toward them more than any other factor, and people reflect your attitude right back at you, like a mirror, whether positive or negative.

– Courtesy of Jim Rohn

Get a life in which **you are not alone.** Find people you love, **and who love you.** And remember that love is not leisure, **it is work.**

— Anna Quindlen

Choose **EXCELLENCE.**
Choose **TO BE THE BEST.**
Choose **GOOD HEALTH.**
Choose **HAPPINESS.**
Choose **WELL.**

IT'S YOUR CHOICE!

— Myers Barnes

**Success is not for those who want it,
nor those who need it,
but for those who are utterly determined to seize it –
whatever it takes.**

– Darren Hardy

you would never think a
negative thought.
– Peace Pilgrim

Winners, I am convinced, imagine their dreams first. They want it with all their heart and expect it to come true. **There is, I believe, no other way to live.**

– Joe Montana

EXPECT PROBLEMS AND EAT THEM FOR BREAKFAST.

– Alfred A. Montapert

IT'S YOUR LIFE.
YOU ARE RESPONSIBLE FOR YOUR RESULTS.

IT'S TIME TO TURN UP
THE HEAT.

– SAM PARKER

If you have *zest* and *enthusiasm* you attract *zest* and *enthusiasm*. Life does give back in kind.

– Norman Vincent Peale

MOST PEOPLE SETTLE FOR GOOD ENOUGH.

WHAT THE HELL IS "GOOD ENOUGH?"

THERE'S ALWAYS BETTER.

— DARREN HARDY

YOUR CONFIDENCE WILL LEAD YOU TO SUCCESS.

–Panda Express Fortune Cookie

WWW.BETTERHUMAN.TODAY

It's about striving to be **better,**
and sharing it with the world.

Visit Elevate for our latest offerings:
www.elevatepub.com